The Life of
Benjamin Franklin
An American Original

Yona Zeldis McDonough

paintings by Malcah Zeldis

Henry Holt and Company

New York

Henry Holt and Company, LLC
Publishers since 1866
175 Fifth Avenue, New York, New York 10010
www.henryholtchildrensbooks.com

Library of Congress Cataloging-in-Publication Data
McDonough, Yona Zeldis.
The life of Benjamin Franklin : an American original / by Yona Zeldis McDonough ;
paintings by Malcah Zeldis.
p.   cm.
ISBN-13: 978-0-8050-7856-5
ISBN-10: 0-8050-7856-8
1. Franklin, Benjamin, 1706–1790—Juvenile literature. 2. Statesmen—United States—
Biography—Juvenile literature. 3. Inventors—United States—Biography—Juvenile literature.
4. Scientists—United States—Biography—Juvenile literature. 5. Printers—United States—
Biography—Juvenile literature. I. Zeldis, Malcah, ill. II. Title.
E302.6.F8M13 2006   973.3'092—dc22   2005012130
First Edition—2006 / Designed by Donna Mark
Printed in China

1 3 5 7 9 10 8 6 4 2

The artist used gouache on paper to create
the illustrations for this book.

For my brother, David Zeldis

—Y. Z. M.

To my dear friend Annette Miller

—M. Z.

*T*he two men walked quickly down the street, eyes fixed on the storm clouds overhead. One held an unusual kite—it had a metal wire sticking out of the top and a metal house key attached to its string. The men reached a field as the rain began. Lightning flashed. The younger man ran across the field and the kite soared upward. The older man took the string, and, dripping wet, the two went into a shed to wait. For a few minutes, nothing happened. They looked at each other, disappointed. Then the man holding the string noticed that its fibers were standing up and apart, as if they had come alive. He put his knuckle near the key and felt a tingle—an electric shock! Just as he had hoped, a spark from the storm cloud had traveled down the wet string into the metal key, electrifying it. The tingle was the proof. The man's name was Benjamin Franklin, and with the help of his son William, he had demonstrated that lightning and electricity were the very same thing.

Benjamin Franklin was born on a freezing day in 1706. His father, Josiah, made soap and candles in the colonial city of Boston; his mother, Abiah, took care of the other children— there were thirteen! They all lived in a tiny, four-room house. Ben learned to read early and spent many winter afternoons curled up with a book. His parents were not rich, so they had few books, but Ben didn't mind; he read the same ones over and over, even though they contained big words and scarcely any pictures.

When he was seven, he wrote a poem. This was so unusual that his parents sent him to school. Not every child went to school; being chosen was an honor. Ben excelled at reading and handwriting, but he failed arithmetic and didn't understand why he should study Latin, an ancient language no one spoke. He grew into a strong, sturdy boy with curly hair and big clear eyes. He loved kite flying and swimming; his first idea for an invention was to slip four paddles over his hands and feet so he could swim faster.

After two years, Ben had to leave school to help his parents in the shop. Ben hated the smell of the tallow—fat from sheep and cows—used in candles even more than he hated arithmetic. Josiah Franklin began looking around for other work his son could do. Carpentry? Bricklaying? Brass-working? Nothing appealed to Ben. Finally, Josiah had what he thought was a brilliant idea: Since Ben liked books so much, why not learn to make them?

Ben was apprenticed to his older brother, James, who had a printing shop in Boston. Ben didn't want to work for James, but it was better than laying bricks. So in 1718, at the age of twelve, Ben began his life as a printer-in-training.

In James's shop, Ben learned to set type, placing tiny metal letters in special frames so they could be used to print the words on paper. Before long he was printing booklets and songs. Ben also tried his hand at writing. He wrote a poem about a famous drowning and another about the pirate Blackbeard. James liked Ben's poems enough to print them. Soon the people of Boston were talking about the boy poet. In 1721, James started his own newspaper, the *New England Courant*. Ben printed and delivered copies. He liked the job, but he didn't like James, who was a harsh master.

Ben began writing funny pieces about life in Boston. Taking on the character of a widow, he signed the pieces with the name he had invented for her, Silence Dogood, and slipped them under the door of the shop. James believed Silence Dogood was real and printed those, too. Everyone wanted to know the identity of Silence Dogood. When Ben revealed himself as the author, people were amused. Except James. He was angry. But James had other problems. He had printed critical articles about the English officials who ran the state. First this landed him in jail, and then it lost him his job—he was forbidden to publish the paper. James thought he could get around this by making Ben the publisher and secretly maintaining control. But Ben didn't want to do it. The brothers fought bitterly, and Ben ran away.

Ben arrived in Philadelphia hungry, tired, and dirty. He bought three rolls for a penny each at a bakery and stuffed one into his mouth. The other two went under each arm because his pockets were full. As he chewed, a girl standing in a doorway started to laugh. Her name was Deborah Read; soon Ben was renting a room from her family. He found a job with a printer, who quickly put him in charge of the business. The governor of Philadelphia was impressed with Ben's work, too, and offered to set him up in business. Ben would go to England to buy a printing press and other supplies. The governor would pay the bills.

Eighteen-year-old Ben was excited to set sail; he left for London in 1724. But the governor had lied—the money and letters of introduction never came. Ben was more than three thousand miles from home and penniless. He managed to get a job in a London print shop. He stayed until he had enough money to go home.

Once Ben returned, he got back his old job in the print shop. It wasn't long before he was able to start his own business. By 1729, he was publishing a newspaper, the *Pennsylvania Gazette*. Ben was the printer, editor, and top reporter. The paper also ran jokes, riddles, and letters to the editor. If there weren't enough letters, Ben wrote them himself, signing them with invented names. He drew what was probably the first cartoon to appear in an American paper.

By this time, Ben had a son, William, whose mother was never named. But he married Deborah Read, the girl who had laughed when she saw him carrying rolls under his arms. Deborah (or Debby, as he called her) helped Ben run the print shop and store—filled with stationery, pens, ink, candles, and books—that he opened next door. Ben and Debby had two children, Franky and Sally. When Franky was four, he caught smallpox and died. Ben grieved for months.

With Debby's help, Ben's printing business became highly successful. In 1732, he was able to launch *Poor Richard's Almanack*. Almanacs offer dates of holidays, seasons, fairs, court openings, and weather forecasts, as well as tides, phases of the moon, and eclipses. Ben's almanac included these and more: He wrote it under the name of Richard Saunders and filled it with tidbits about his life, comic advice, and witty sayings. "Pay what you owe, and what you're worth you'll know" was one. "Haste makes waste" and "A penny saved is a penny earned" were others. The almanac became wildly popular and turned its author into a rich man. Ben no longer had to work as a printer, so he put his business in the hands of a partner. Ben was just forty-two and had energy to burn.

Ben had long wanted to improve life in Philadelphia. His love of books had prompted him to help establish the country's first lending library in 1731. He helped found the first fire department, made up of thirty volunteers, in 1736. He had urged the city's government to light and pave the muddy streets and to have them cleaned. In 1751, he supported the establishment of the country's first hospital, which was in Philadelphia.

Four years later, Ben helped found an academy for young people, which would later become the University of Pennsylvania; part of the academy was a free school for poor children. Ben had already been named postmaster in 1737, and English officials made him deputy postmaster general for America in 1753. Now Ben could hire more letter carriers and establish improved mail routes. In so many ways, he made things better for people in the city and the colonies.

Ben had always loved science. When he and William made their amazing discovery about the nature of electricity in 1752, word traveled quickly. Everyone was excited by what Ben had done. But Ben asked, "What good is philosophy that does not apply to some use?" He wanted to make lightning less dangerous and had an idea how he could do it. A metal rod was attached to the top of a building with a wire running down the side of the building to the ground. When a bolt of lightning hit, electricity ran harmlessly through the wire and into the ground. The building and the people in it remained safe.

Ben put a lightning rod on his own house. Soon, many other buildings, including the state capitol of Maryland in Annapolis, added lightning rods. Yet Ben refused to patent his invention or to profit from it. Instead, he published a detailed description of his lightning rod, so that anyone who wanted to could install one.

Ben put his interest in science to work in all kinds of practical projects. He invented a heating device known as the Franklin stove that directed heat from a fireplace into a room, rather than up and out the chimney. He devised a more efficient, long-burning lamp for the city streets. As he grew older, he needed two pairs of eyeglasses—one to read, the other for distance—so he combined them into a single frame called bifocals. Millions of people still wear these today. He played the violin, harp, and guitar and invented the "glass armonica," which used different-sized glass bowls spun on a cradle.

Politics was another area that interested Ben. In 1736, he had been chosen as the clerk of Pennsylvania's Assembly, the legislative body that met in Philadelphia. For fifteen years, he recorded debates and votes. Yet, "I was at length tired with sitting there to hear debates, in which, as clerk, I could take no part." In 1751, he ran for a seat in the Assembly and won.

Three years later, in 1754, the French and Indian War broke
out. This war was about who would control North America.
France, aided by her Indian allies, was on one side. Britain,
aided by the thirteen colonies, was on the other. Ben served as
a British colonel. William helped, too. They led soldiers, built
forts, and organized patrols. Still, the colonies needed more
money to fight the war, and in 1757, Ben and William went
to England to raise it. Their journey was a hard one. They were
almost captured by French pirates. They ran into storms and
were nearly shipwrecked.

Finally, they reached London, where Ben spent five years raising money for the war while William studied law. Ben enjoyed the attention he received as America's foremost scientist and inventor. William was named royal governor of New Jersey by King George III of England and got married. In 1762, Ben went home to Philadelphia; the newlyweds returned to America soon afterward.

Trouble was brewing at home. The Penns, the English family who had founded Pennsylvania, still ruled the colony. Many of the colonists wanted to be under the direct rule of the king. In 1764, Ben was sent back to London to make this happen. He was there only a short time when an even more serious problem arose. England, who had won the French and Indian War, was now deeply in debt. To raise money, England passed the Stamp Act in early 1765. The new law taxed Americans on newspapers and other paper goods.

Ben was against the tax, but not very strongly. He didn't know that enraged colonists back home were protesting it. They thought Ben had betrayed them and threatened to burn down his Philadelphia house.

Ben learned of this and quickly realized how angry the Americans were. He voiced his opposition to the Stamp Act and fought against it by writing to newspapers, debating with lawmakers, and making speeches. The tax was repealed, in large part because of Ben's efforts. But the British responded by taxing other items, such as tea. In the past, Ben had felt like an Englishman living in America. Now he began to see things differently. The English did not treat the people living in the colonies as equals. They taxed them but did not let them vote.

In December 1774, William wrote to his father that Deborah Franklin, Ben's wife of forty-four years, had died. Ben set sail for home in March of 1775. He was heartsick. His wife was gone, and he felt his mission in England had failed. On April 19, while Ben's boat was still at sea, war broke out between England and the colonies.

Ben arrived in Philadelphia on May 5, 1775, and started his work in the Continental Congress the very next day. The Congress was a group of American leaders whose main purpose

was to win the war against England. At sixty-nine, Ben was not young, yet he worked twelve hours a day. As postmaster, it was up to him to make the mail move quickly. He also tried to convince the Canadians, who were ruled by the English, to side with America. Ben was not successful in winning the Canadians over, and the long, hard trip north nearly killed him. Still, he made it back to Philadelphia, where the Congress was debating a crucial question: Should America declare its independence from England?

Some people thought that once the tax issues were resolved, America could return to British rule. Others felt it was time to form a new nation. If the decision were made for independence, America would need to explain why she wanted to break away from England. In June 1776, Congress asked five men to write a Declaration of Independence; Benjamin Franklin was one of them. Congress put the question to a vote on July 2, 1776. Ben was a very persuasive speaker. A vote was taken: Independence was the winner. Two days later, Congress approved the Declaration and ever since, July 4 has been celebrated as the birthday of the new nation.

Thrilled as Ben was, he regretted that William supported England. No amount of pleading would change his mind. Then William was thrown in jail. Ben could have asked Congress to free him, but with America in such danger, he did not want to ask for special favors—even for his own son.

War raged on. At first it looked like the British might win. Then Congress asked Ben to persuade the French to join America's cause. Ben was an old man now. A trip to France would not be easy. But he went. Winter storms buffeted his ship. British spies were everywhere. Ben had to write messages in invisible ink and sign them with a secret code name.

This time, Ben succeeded. The French joined the Americans, and America won the war in 1783. Ben wanted to go home after the peace treaty between Britain and America was signed, but Congress asked him to stay as ambassador to France. He didn't leave until 1785. William had been set free during the war and was living in England when Ben came through the country on his way home. William visited his father, hoping to make up, but Ben refused. He could not forgive William for siding with the British.

Back in Philadelphia, Ben was treated like a hero. A short time later, he was elected president of the Supreme Executive Council of Pennsylvania. At the age of eighty-one, he helped write the United States Constitution. The Constitution was signed on September 17, 1787, and is still one of the most important expressions of the ruling ideals of the country.

Since returning from England, Ben had been living with his daughter and his grandchildren. His health had begun to decline. When confined to his bed, he liked to listen to the older ones recite their lessons.

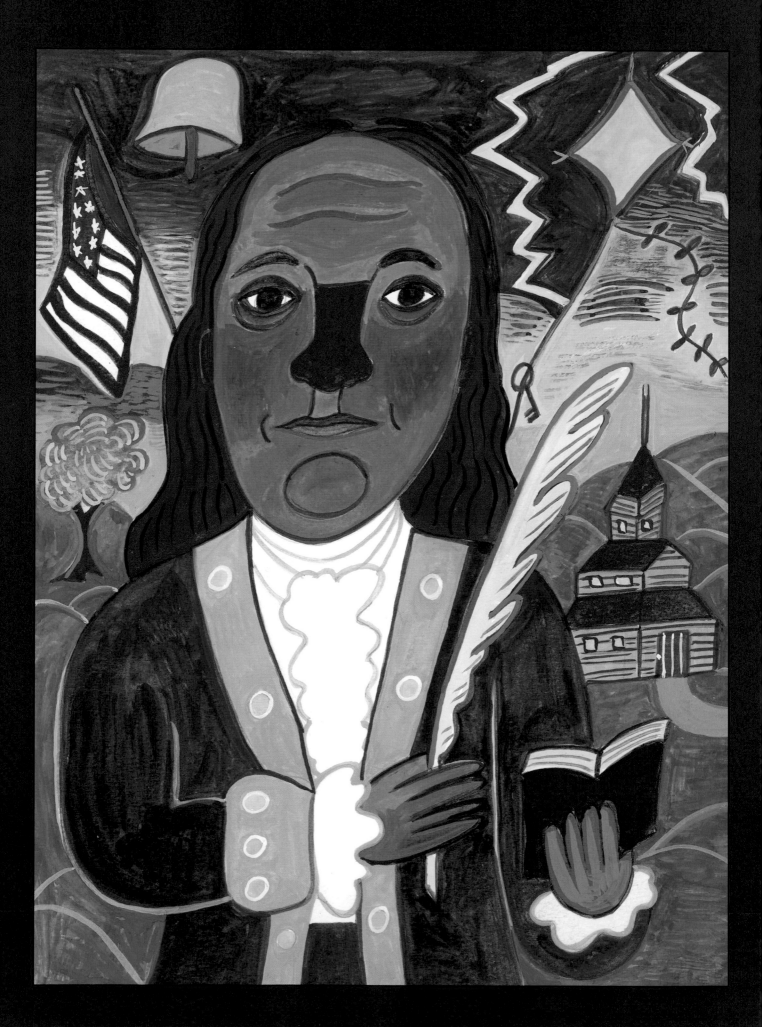

One of the last things Ben did was to try to outlaw slavery. He was the president of an antislavery society and published his views. One of his final public acts was to petition Congress to end the practice.

In the spring of 1790, Ben became sick, and on April 17, he died at the age of eighty-four. The country and the world mourned him. More than twenty thousand people gathered at his funeral. After his death, tributes kept pouring in. Poems, articles, and books were written; statues erected. His name has graced the streets and institutions of countless American cities, and his face—wise and kind—still smiles out from the hundred-dollar bill. Although he lived long ago, his influence—as a printer, writer, scientist, inventor, patriot, and statesman—is still felt, and the great country he helped to create has continued to prosper and grow.

Time Line of Benjamin Franklin's Life

1706 Born on Milk Street, in Boston.

1718 Apprenticed to his brother James for eight years without pay.

1722 Publishes humorous articles under the name Silence Dogood.

1723 Runs away, first to New York and then to Philadelphia; meets future wife, Debby Read.

1724 Sails to England for the first time.

1726 Returns to Philadelphia.

1728 Opens a print shop in Philadelphia.

1730 First son, William, is born; marries Debby.

1731 Plans and starts the first lending library in America.

1732 Publishes *Poor Richard's Almanack*; second son, Franky, is born.

1736 Organizes first volunteer fire brigade in Philadelphia; Franky dies of smallpox.

1737 Appointed postmaster of Philadelphia.

1743 Daughter, Sally, is born.

1751 Elected to the Pennsylvania Assembly.

1752 Performs his experiment with kite, key, and lightning.

1757 Sails for England again.

1762 Returns to Philadelphia for a short stay; sails back to England two years later.

1766 Fights for the repeal of the Stamp Act.

1771 Begins writing what is known today as *The Autobiography of Benjamin Franklin*.

1774 Wife, Debby, dies; returns to Philadelphia; appointed to the Second Continental Congress.

1776 Chosen to help write the Declaration of Independence; sails to France to seek support for America.

1783 Helps draw up peace treaty between United States and England.

1785 Receives a hero's welcome when he returns home.

1787 Signs the United States Constitution at age eighty-one, the oldest man to do so.

1789 Appointed president of an antislavery society.

1790 Dies on April 17.

Inventions of Benjamin Franklin

Bifocal glasses or **double spectacles** combined distance and close-vision lenses in a single pair of glasses.

The Busybody consisted of two or three mirrors strategically placed above and next to a door. It enabled a person sitting on the second floor of a house to see who was at the door without having to go downstairs to open the door.

Clock with three wheels showed hours, minutes, and seconds; prior to this, American clocks showed only hours and minutes.

Extension arm, a long pole with a pair of pincers at the end, was used to grab items on high shelves.

Franklin stove spread hot air evenly throughout a room, while directing smoke up and out through the chimney.

Library chair had steps concealed beneath it; they could be pulled out and used for climbing to reach a book on a high shelf.

Lightning rod was used to attract lightning and safely divert it away from buildings and people.

Remote-control lock was designed so a person could lock the door from bed using a rope and pulley.

Sayings from _Poor Richard's Almanack_

(All these sayings appeared in the almanac; some Ben invented, and others he adapted and rephrased.)

Fish and visitors smell in three days.

God helps them that helps themselves.

Three may keep a secret if two of them are dead.

Men and melons are hard to know.

He that goes a borrowing goes a sorrowing.

Little strokes fell great oaks.

Lost time is never found again.

If you would be loved, love and be lovable.

An apple a day keeps the doctor away.

He that lieth down with dogs shall rise up with fleas.

The greatest talkers are the least doers.

Early to bed, early to rise, makes a man healthy, wealthy, and wise.

The doors of wisdom are never shut.

Bibliography

Adler, David A. B. Franklin, Printer. New York: Holiday House, 2001.

Cousins, Margaret. Ben Franklin of Old Philadelphia. New York: Random House, 1952.

Davidson, Margaret. The Story of Benjamin Franklin, Amazing American. New York: Yearling Books, 1988.

Fleming, Candace. Ben Franklin's Almanac. New York: Atheneum, 2003.

Foster, Leila Merrell. Benjamin Franklin: Founding Father and Inventor. Springfield, NJ: Enslow Publishers, 1997.

Fradin, Dennis Brindell. Who Was Ben Franklin? New York: Grosset & Dunlap, 2002.

Giblin, James Cross. The Amazing Life of Benjamin Franklin. New York: Scholastic Press, 2000.

Van Doren, Carl. Benjamin Franklin. New York: Penguin Books, 1938.